God Bless You,
Lexi

Windows to
My Heart

Judy L. Creel

Windows to My Heart

JUDY L CREEL

Library of Congress Control Number: 2014909058
ISBN: Hardcover   978-1-4990-1952-0
               Softcover   978-1-4990-1953-7
               eBook   978-1-4990-1951-3

This book was printed in the United States of America.

Rev. date: 06/24/2014

To order additional copies of this book, contact:
Xlibris LLC
1-888-795-4274
www.Xlibris.com
Orders@Xlibris.com
603725

This book is dedicated to my mother, Dorothy Beveridge and her friend Colleen Hooks (both now in Heaven) for their encouragement. Also to my husband, Gary and my daughter, Marci Lyn for their support.

CONTENTS

BIRTHDAY

God has enhanced your world with little twin boys
Their lives will hold so, so many precious joys

Rachel and Ryan, God has blessed you from above
Bestowing these sweet, wonderful babies to love

The pride and satisfaction of being a parent is amazing
And yes, some events with boys will be hair-raising

Relax, pray, and enjoy the moments through the years
Always remember there will be laughter and tears

There will be happiness and many things to share
Nothing else on this earth will ever compare!

It is again that one time of the year
When a very special birthday is here

As you blow out the candles on your cake
Remember, it's your turn a wish to make

It may be a dream of financial wealth
Or better yet, for good physical health

Maybe you long for contentment and peace
Or simply for a burden to decrease

Whatever are the desires in your heart
We pray that our God to you will impart!

JUDY L CREEL

As the trumpets blare
News to the world to share
Your birthday is today
And we all want to say
Hope your special day is fun for you
Enjoying the things you like to do!

Even though you're a year older
You're welcome to cry on my shoulder
True friends are there through thick and thin
And stay by their side whether they lose or win
The closeness that develops through the years
Has helped to wipe away many tears
We've laughed, we've cried, we've shared
It was important to know someone cared
Friends we are and friends we'll stay
Until we enter Heaven's Gates one day!

JUDY L CREEL

It's time to celebrate
With ice cream and cake
Gifts and party hats
Baseballs and wooden bats
Crayons, books, and dolls
Pictures hung on the walls
Colorful balloons and red-nosed clowns
The fun and excitement is all around
My head's in a spin
So let the party begin!

This is your very own special day
To be enjoyed in your very own special way
Take time to smell the pretty flowers
Making the most of your birthday hours
Savor the cake and candy
Enjoy a birthday that's *dandy*!

Birthdays are a good time to reflect
Our paths if needed to redirect
Dreams of ours to reconsider
Not to let them die or wither
Unfinished plans to fulfill
Praying for God's perfect will
May God's blessings abound
It's so nice to have you around!

Happy birthday to you, our friend
To you best wishes we extend
We thank God for your special day
Enjoy the moments your chosen way
Remember we do truly care
These sentiments we wanted to share!

Another candle on your cake
Another year to celebrate
Another time to thank God above
For His gift of Eternal Love
He's protected you through the years
And wiped away many tears
He's provided all for you
Now enjoy your *birthday* too!

Rumor has it—today's your birthday
Can't let this day slip away
Without wishing you a happy day!
Birthdays are a gift from God above
Another way He shows His love
Enjoy the birthday plans for sure
And pray you'll have many more

JUDY L CREEL

Yes, another birthday to celebrate
And another candle on your cake
Another day to thank God above
For His protection and His love
Another day to know you are blessed
And on His promises you can rest
So have a happy, happy day
On this, your very own birthday!

B is for the wonderful Blessing you have been
I is for the Immense joy you bring, Marci Lyn
R is for the Radiance you display in a crowd
T is for the many Times you made us proud
H is for the Happiness you impart
D is for the Desires of your heart
A is for your Active, busy pace in life
Y is for the Years we've shared, *oh so nice*!

JUDY L CREEL

William's Birthday

B is for the *big boy* you've grown to be

I is for the *immense joy* you bring to me

R is for the *roughhousing* with my guy

T is for the *twinkle* in your pretty eyes

H is for the *happiness* you impart

D is for the *desires* in your heart

A is for your *active*, busy pace

Y is for the *years* I've shared your space!

Giana's Birthday

G is for the pretty, pretty *girl* you are

I is for the *image* of a future star

A is for *active* and busy you

N is for *nice* all the way through

A is for *all* you mean to me

Happy birthday to my Sweet Pea

Hey, what do you say?
It's *Gabe's* birthday
It's time to celebrate
With ice cream and cake
Gifts and party hats
Baseballs and wooden bats
Colorful balloons and red-nosed clowns
The fun and excitement is all around
Only once will you be *five*
So let this party come alive!!

It's a special day for *Daily Grace*
The perky one with the cute little face
Her world is busy with energy galore
With many new adventures in store
She is actually *four* going on *sixteen* today
Living life in her own sweet way
Happy birthday, little red-haired girl
We love you lots—that's for sure!

Our little *Rebekah* turns *one*
Let's celebrate and have some fun
Sweet and darling as she can be
She prefers her mommy's lap, you see
Each day is a new adventure to learn
As she explores her world, it's her turn!

Jo Jo, hope your birthday is loads of fun
As you've matured to the ripe old age of *one*
Growing into a sweet little boy
Providing your family with so much joy
With siblings and toys in tow
Into the terrible twos you will surely go
Never could anyone take your place
Glowing with love in your precious face!

My buddy is *one* year old today
And as cute as a button I say
I feel honored when I have you in my care
And truly enjoy the moments we share
You are such a blessing from Heaven above
I pray for you God's guidance and love
Your dad, mom, and brother are so proud of you
And your church buddy thinks you're special too!

Ashleigh is sweet *sixteen* today
So quickly those years have passed away
It's such a special age to be
With so, so much in life to see
Planning your future education
To obtain that hopeful vocation
Soon to be—*oh no*—driving the car
Enabling you to go near and far
Praying God will continue to bless you
With health, happiness, and contentment too
You are the Queen today
And yes, you can have it your way!

JUDY L CREEL

Wow, today gives you birthday *ninety-two*
Behave and don't do anything we wouldn't do
Count your blessings and not your woes
This will keep you thankful and on your toes
Enjoy your family and friends as you celebrate
Savor some ice cream and your favorite cake
Gary and I wanted to say "Happy birthday" to our friend
So to you, *Jim*, best wishes we extend!

Eden Faith King

*E*verything is all new and loads of fun
*D*eveloping to the ripe old age of one
*E*njoying life as a darling little girl
*N*ow let's give this birthday party a whirl!

*F*inding your way in this sometimes hard life
*A*nd knowing loved ones will help in the strife
*I*magining the little star you will always be
*T*elling the whole world your presence to see!
*H*onoring the Lord as you continue to grow

*K*eeping so busy with toys and blanket in tow
*I*nto the terrible twos you will surely go!
*N*ever could anyone take your place
*G*lowing with love in your precious face!

Wishing you a happy birthday today
You make us laugh in your own special way

You're turning fifty-one, Gloria Jean
And still a vital part of the Hilltop Team

Domenic and Hayden bring you reasons for living
You respond with special care and unselfish giving

Working two jobs to buy food and pay the bills
Your life as the loving grandma to fulfill

May God reward your special day from above
With happiness, health, and His wonderful *love*!

Wow, can you believe it's birthday twenty-three
You have a daughter and a full-time job, you see

Living with PJ and building your life together
Holding on as the storms of life you weather

Enjoy your birthday with ice cream and cake
And behave yourself for Heaven's sake!

May God reward your special day from above
With happiness, health, and His wonderful *love*!

Just wanted to wish you a happy fifty-fifth birthday
Please enjoy your day in a very special way

Reflect on the blessings and not the trials
Let life's concerns fly away for a while

Our paths did not cross just by a chance in time
It was destined by God's perfect plan and design

As a bank teller I met you years ago
Then as a coworker, a friend I got to know

Friendships grow over conversations and time
I thank God that you are a friend of mine!

May your future hold contentment and health
Neither of which can be purchased with wealth

Frank, sixty years have come and gone
You probably can't say you've done no wrong

But you have experienced good health
And amassed some knowledge and some wealth

You've been surrounded by family and love
Reasons to thank God for blessings from above

To still have your parents is so neat
Their wisdom to share is such a treat

Sports and grandchildren bring enjoyment to your life
A companion by your side is your devoted wife

We appreciate your S&T loyalty through the ranks
For your willingness to help us, *we all say*
                    thanks!

JUDY L CREEL

Jennifer is celebrating birthday number thirty-four
May your special day hold good things in store

The last few years have gone so fast
As we have actively fulfilled our tasks

Memories of your engagement and then marriage
Followed by Jaisa and Joey to fill the baby carriage

Career changes were made by switching offices for work
And the promise of a title was always the extra perk

It was my pleasure to have you on my staff for a while
You were always willing to go that extra mile

It was in God's divine plan that our paths would one day meet
Getting to know you and share in your life has been a treat

I wish you a happy birthday for sure
And pray God gives you many more!

Yes, Kathy turns fifty-three today
Celebrate this birthday your chosen way

Have some ice cream and birthday cake
And behave yourself for goodness' sake

You have been with the bank for eight long years
I am positive there have been good days and tears

Treat yourself today with some good enjoyment
Remember we met through our bank employment

Nothing happens by mere chance in time
God knew one day our paths would align

I truly enjoyed the days we picked hair off toads
Performing that task took us down many roads

I am sure in time we will meet again
Until then, best wishes I do extend!

Vanessa turns fifty-six this workday
Just a kind warning to not go astray

We met while working at Manor Branch
But nothing just happens by mere chance

It was God's perfect design
That our paths would one day align

We connected with a love of dogs and cats
And of course our discussions and daily chats

You were a real asset on my front line
Very accurate and always on time

In due process you joined the Ford City team
And once again I too became part of the scene

Life has its twists and turns, we've discovered
Many events in our lives have been uncovered

As God continues to measure out years for your enjoyment
Never forget that we met through our bank employment

A happy birthday I want to extend
And best wishes to you, my friend

Happy Birthday
Wow, today God gives you birthday *ninety-four*
Another year with blessings in store!
Enjoy your family and friends as you celebrate
Savor some ice cream and a piece of cake.

Erma

*E*very day is a gift from God above
*R*emembering His great blessing of love.
*M*ay this birthday be one of your very best
*A*nd the days to follow bring you health, peace, and rest!

Dominique

*D*uring your lifetime you have been happy and sad
*O*vercoming heartaches allows good to conquer bad.
*M*arrying Brian, the soul mate of your life
*I*dentifying yourselves as husband and wife.
*N*ourishing William and Giana with love
*I*s such a special blessing from God above.
*Q*uitting the single life offered joys untold
*U*plifting moments and events to forever hold
*E*nvisioning only the best as more years unfold!

Janice

*J*ust because you turn "seventy" today
*A*ct on any dreams you've hid away
*N*othing is impossible if we press on
*I*f we quit or give up, they will be gone
*C*oncentrate on the blessings that are sent
*E*njoy everyday to the fullest extent!

Nancy

*N*ot a soul could ever take your place
*A*lways having a smile on your face
*N*ever letting life's trials be your defeat
*C*aring for family and those you meet
*Y*ou deserve your birthday to be a treat!

Debi

*D*o not ever, ever dismiss your heartfelt dreams
*E*nvision only success in all of life schemes
*B*e confident in the person you've become
*I*nvestments in character will never be undone!

Debi

*D*own the tubes goes another year
*E*very laughter and every tear
*B*lessings await this brand new year
*I*ndeed with God no need to fear!

CINDY

*C*asting all your worries and fears aside
*I*t is your birthday, so enjoy the ride
*N*o more do we work as Fric and Frac
*D*uties that caused us to cringe and laugh
*Y*ears that long ago came to an end

*L*eaving memories in the mind of a friend
*A*s life has given us heartaches to bear
*W*e still have our precious friendship to share!

MARY ALICE

*M*ay your birthday be a special treat
*A*s you remember memories sweet
*R*ecalling the good times in your life
*Y*et overcoming issues of strife

*A*lways be thankful for family and friends
*L*iving each day as a gift God extends
*I*ndeed be happy for blessings He sends
*C*elebrating good events as time affords
*E*nvisioning more years as God rewards!

Happy Birthday

Wednesday is a special day for Ida Mae
God blessed her with ninety years that day
Her life has been shared with two husbands and two sons
Some of which God has called to their home above
One son remains, Roger Lee, you see
Roxie, her daughter-in-law and grandsons three
Two great-grandchildren finish the family tree
(And of course all of her friends, including you and me)
The little village of Cadogan is where she calls home
Some days are long as she lives there all alone
Her niece Hally helps her in so many ways
Shopping, doctor appointments, and various errands each day
In her lifetime she has seen many new inventions
Enough technology and gizmos to get anyone's attention
As God continues to measure out more years from above
We pray for contentment, health, and rest in God's Love.

Belated Happy Birthday

Missing your birthday was such a mistake
I hope you enjoyed your ice cream and cake

How I missed May 20 as your special day
To let this slip by—what can I say?

Sorry seems so lame and cold
I guess I'm getting way too *old*

Truly hope your birthday was a lot of fun
Until next year that celebration is done

JUDY L CREEL

EVENTS

BEACH

Off to the beach for a day in the sun
Nothing but awesome hours of pure fun
Not a cloud in the big, clear, blue sky
To not go more often I wonder why
With our sunglasses, lawn chairs and sunscreen
My buddies and I make a good beach team
The race is on as we approach the shore
Jump in the water and make splashes galore
Grab the surf board and ride the ocean waves
Big waves or little ones don't seem to phase
We all share the warm wind in our face
No where on earth is there a better place
Back to the beach to suntan and rest
Building sand castles to win the best
Gathering sea shells along the shoreline
Haven't had this much fun in a long time!

FAIR

With a breeze and a nip in the air
Our family is scrambling to attend the fair
The ferris wheel rises high to the sky
The merry go round catches our eye
The bumper cars make much noise as they crash
The magician makes things disappear in a flash
Aromas from food booths permeate the air
While the auctioneer peddles his wares
New farm machinery all clean and bright
In hopes a farmer will buy one on sight
Down to the cow, sheep and horse barns
And produce displays that come from the farms
Baked pies, cakes and canned goods in a row
Ribbons and stars awarded to best in show
Local talent puts on an act hard to beat
We see many neighbors and friends to greet
The local fair offers much to behold
To people of any age, young or old!

PARK

We are going to the playground at the park
Grandma says we can stay there until dark
With sand bucket and toy truck in tow
It is now off to the park we go
Into the sand box with the other girls and boys
And we play in the sand and share our toys
The birds are flying above our heads
As the warm sun shines on the flowerbeds
The little pond is filled with lots of fish
So we throw in pennies and make a wish
We run to the swing set across the yard
Safety first as we are watched by the guard
Up the steps and down the slippery slide
Up and down on the see saw, I giggled inside
Into the jumping tent filled with screams and laughs
I thanked Grandma for the fun on my behalf!

Zoo

Awake, awake little sleepy head
We have a big, busy day ahead
Wash my face and brush my tousled hair
Decisions, decisions about what to wear
Bathroom chores and my dressing now done
Anxiously awaiting this day of fun
Cereal and juice to start the day
Now brush my teeth and we're on our way
My Dad, My Mom, my sister and me
All pile in the mini van, you see
Finally at the zoo with tickets in hand
We watch the clowns doing headstands
Off to the monkeys swinging from tree to tree
The giraffe has a long neck, we all agree
Next are the otters frolicking in the pool
Enormous gray elephants, so cool
Striped tigers all pace in their cage
While big lions roar in a rage
Tall guys all walking on stilts take the show
How they stand I guess I will never know
Various colorful birds flying in the air
Corn dogs and cotton candy to share
Then to the aquarium with noses to the glass
With so much to see, time went so fast
Loading back in the van with heads in a spin
Good memories to last till we come again!

PRESCHOOL GRADUATION

WOW, you've learned your ABC's
And how to count 1 2 3!
Shapes, colors and new words unfurled
Some little friends entered your world
Such a big, sweet boy you've become
In Grandma's eyes you're number one
Preschool was so much fun you see
Now off to kindergarten you will be,
With all your hard work, GEE Wheeez
You've earned a day at Chuck-E-Cheese!

GET WELL

Welcome to the World of Hospital

Everywhere you look at the sights
Doctors and nurses dressed in whites

Meet the cool, drafty bedgowns
Tubes and hoses wrapped all around

There's the wobbly bedpan shaped like a wreath
And that uncomfortable bed lump underneath

Jello and broths are favored meals
Served from the carts with noisy wheels

Shots, pills, and blood-pressure cuffs
Cold thermometers stuck up your duff

Hurry and get better with a good health scheme
And your stay will be over like a bad dream

Get-well prayers for you, my friend
A speedy recovery to you we extend

Get-Well Verses

1. Eat prunes.
2. Drink plenty of liquids.
3. Stay in bed and rest.

Ah—wait—that may not work?
Can't wait to hear the doc's diagnosis,
"All is well."

Prayers and best wishes
Are being sent your way
Trust they will work
To bring you a good day!
Get well soon

Take the doctor's advice—be real nice
Endure that shot—swallow that pill
Strut around in that show-all gown
Before you know it—you'll be out on the town
Best wishes for a speedy recovery

JUDY L CREEL

A speedy recovery and a short hospital stay
Would be an answer to our prayers today
Get well soon and stay that way
Would make for a happy day

Pray your illness is brief
And you'll soon get relief
This will allow you a much-needed rest
In no time at all, you'll be back at your best
These would be the desires of our heart
If our prayers are answered on your part
    Get well soon

JUDY L CREEL

May your aches and pains go down the drain
The soreness and hurts can do the same
Let those hospital bills vanish away
In hopes that you will have a good day

Pray your toe is feeling better today
And will no longer get in your way
Pray your recovery will be fast
And the dreadful pain will be past
Pray God will heal your sore toe
And through this His love will show

Pray you will feel better each day
So you can be out on your way
Living your life to the fullest
This scenario would be the coolest
Anything we can do to help ease your stay
Remember, we are just a phone call away!
Get well soon

We are asking God for your cure
Being sick is not pleasant for sure

Please be a good patient and obey
Hence make this a short hospital stay

May your medical team be the very best
Until you're well, try to benefit from the rest

Waiting to hear the good news at last
That your sick days are part of your past!

JUDY L CREEL

Stop the endless cough and runny nose
Get out of bed and on your toes

Be brave, strong and take those meds
Let them rid the snot and clear your head

Fever gone and throat not sore
Now enjoy your life once more

These steps will help you mend
That's what we recommend!

Lying alone in your bed
With an ice pack on your head

Swallowing liquids and pills
In hopes it will cure your ills

Our prayers are with you, poor soul
With wishes you'll soon be whole!

JUDY L CREEL

Knowing that you are feeling bad
Makes us and many people sad

Listen to the doctor's prediction
On the way to rid your affliction

The staff wants to help you heal
And obeying is the best deal

As God works on your condition
You will resume your life's position

We look forward to that day
You are healed and on your way

Good health to you, our friend
Best wishes until then

It is no fun being sick
Hurry, get well real quick!
Swallow your meds each day
Obey what the doc has to say
Soon you will be good as new
Doing those things you like to do!

JUDY L CREEL

Feelin' kinda sad and blue
Not likin' what you're goin' through?
Sometimes rest is good, it's been said
But it's never fun to be sick in bed!
So enough of this lyin' around
Time to rise up and visit the town
Don't let days of life pass away
Get better soon and stay that way!

So sorry to hear you're under the weather
Waiting for the day that you're all better
Pray God will guide the procedures from the start
And for the hospital staff His guidance impart
Then for his power of healing to restore
That your sick days will be no more

JUDY L CREEL

Praying you will get better really quick
It is never a good thing to be sick

We hope the nurses take good care of you
And that the doctors will know what to do

Taking advice is oft against our will
Yes, you must definitely take that pill

And when you face that needle eye-to-eye
Just take the shot with an ouch and a sigh

Truly hope sickness is soon a part of your past
And physical healing for you will be quite fast

Looking forward to hear a good health report
Until then, we are here for needed support

Inform us if there is anything we can do
We certainly do not want you to be blue

Get well soon.

I have been thinking of you both today
Sorry for the trials that have come your way.
It is hard to understand the events of life
And so difficult to endure unwanted strife.
My prayer is for God to give you strength and peace
And that His will would include some pain relief.
I have been praying for Jim's breathing troubles
And for wisdom for you to handle the struggles.
Someday I am sure we will understand all our woes
Until then we know God is in control as life goes!

JUDY L CREEL

I am thrilled to hear you are cancer-free
You go girl that's the way to be!

It has been a long, hard road
And never easy to bear the load

Praise God for His answer to prayer
Knowing you were always in His care

It is wonderful he saw fit to give the cure
And I know you appreciate it for sure

Hope you can enjoy life a little more
With many good things for the future in store!

Life's trials are so difficult to bear
Seems you have had more than your share.

Heard you had to leave your profession
Probably was a hard choice, I'm guessin'.

Praying your doctor will find a cure for you
And I'm asking God to bless you too!

JUDY L CREEL

CHILD'S GET-WELL VERSES

You're sick? ☹ Oh no, it cannot be
I'll count my ears, one, two, three
Then I'll jump and fall on my knees
I'll try to say all my ABCs
Then I'll dance and sing
I'll even shout and scream
But wait! I'll ask God above
To provide his healing love
God will hear my prayer for sure
And I'll thank him for your cure

Got the word you're in bed and sick
Ask God to make you well real quick
Can't have our little buddy ill
With a temperature and a chill
Enough crying with a tummy ache
Get better, for goodness' sake!
We love you and want you healed
Then our hearts will be so thrilled!

JUDY L CREEL

LIFE'S
REFLECTIONS

LIFE

Life holds so, so many twists and turns
Solving problems and handling concerns

Sometimes we think the world should have to stop
This merry-go-round needs to let us off

We need time to smell the flowers
An overwhelming urge to savor our hours

All the hustle and bustle of life
We want a break from all the strife

We're prone to gain possessions and wealth
Many times at the expense of our health

Only in the end to leave it all behind
None of it in the hereafter to find

Only as we serve and help others will treasures be stored
By the only ONE who honestly keeps the scoreboard

Help us remember this is but a training base
For an eternity that can be ours in Heaven's place

The fee for entrance has been paid
At the cross of Jesus our sins were laid

Accept the Lord's payment in full today
Because our life *will* come to an end someday!

LIFE'S BOOK

Slowly the pages of life seem to fold away
But often life seasons become chapters in days

Childhood, school days, careers, and for some, a page of marriage
Chapters, events, and then blessings of a baby carriage

Quickly gone are the pages when children are home
Closing those chapters leave parents feeling alone

Retirement takes on a new chapter for sure
Daily pages of life are changed forevermore

As we reminisce on the chapters of our past
We realize unfinished pages are dwindling fast!

THE DASH

Each of our lives is but a small dash between two dates in time
Our eternity is also determined within this little line

This dash of life can be spent however we choose
But it can only be spent once, so do not misuse

Our dash consists of various experiences and tasks
The moments fade like grains of sand slipping through an hourglass

As we scan a tombstone, it's not the size, color, or design
But the dash that represents how our life will be defined

May our mark on this world be a wonderful blessing and not a scar
That our dash in the memories of others will shine as a bright star

The very second God calls our name, we then are the *I* in die
May our dash be the Hero of our story as we bid good-bye

Please take time to consider the dash of your life's fate
Accept the free gift of salvation before it's *too late*!

As we all journey through this path we call life
We will without exception experience strife

Happiness and sadness, laughing and crying
Business to handle with selling and buying

Some face poverty, and some amass wealth
Everyone has days of sickness and times of health

Good times to enjoy and bad times to endure
We are never really alone for God's presence is sure

Humanly speaking, it's hard to manage these events
So leaning and trusting in God makes perfect sense.

THE PUZZLE

My life is but a puzzle fashioned by God's own hand
At least a zillion pieces designed by God's perfect plan
Often I go astray and make a mess of my pieces
The effectiveness of my perfect puzzle decreases
When obeying the Holy Spirit's leading, I do repent
As far as the east is from the west, the bad pieces are sent
This describes the human cycle of my life every day
As I perform the activities of my earthly stay
Oft times I don't understand the pieces of my life
Then I question, fret, and cause myself much strife
When in essence it's not for me to reason or ask why
The picture of my puzzle will be revealed when I die
Only because of Jesus's redemptive work for me
Will this puzzle be accepted through eternity
Your life is but a puzzle too, my friend
And the master of puzzles has a gift to extend
He died on the cross for everyone's sin
Accept His gift and your puzzle will enter in!

Heartaches

Have you ever been stuck in a stretch of time
When a certain event or action wouldn't leave your mind?

At the occurrence of which left you with unbelief
And the constant replay in your mind has caused much grief.

Especially when you feel in your heart you tried your best
Only to have the results turn out to be a real mess.

Life is often sprinkled with agonizing events
Lessons are to be learned by these hard tests that are sent.

When our own abilities render us too weak to stand
Our coping stamina comes from the Master's outstretched hand.

TRY

Trials

We are depressed and very blue
We hurt and don't know what to do

Not a thing seems to bring us peace
If only this mess could cease

Remember

No such thing as circumstance
Nothing happens just by chance

God's plan included this event
So into our life it was sent

It's not our way but God's that counts
Prayers help us as the heartaches mount

When the answer comes our way
It was for the best, you'll hear us say

Yield

We need to lean on God each day
Instead of insisting on our way

He wants to bestow what's best
That is one reason for the test!

THE RUSH

It appears everyone's in a big hurry—going who knows where in a big scurry

My normal patience is wearing thin—things within my being are in a spin

I'm in need of some peaceful solitude—to alter my unpleasant attitude

Time alone with God's word supreme—true prayers to make my heart clean

Time and mistakes also enable me to see—many events of life won't matter in eternity

The ticket is prepaid to enter Heaven's gate—do not delay acceptance until it's too late

When our death's final call is made—our eternal destination is laid!

CRITTERS

Thank God for creating the critters
Large, medium, and the little lap sitters.

When they look at us through their eyes of love
We truly know they are God's gifts from above.

If I could be the person my pets think I am
My character would really be a grandstand!

Remember to the critters be kind
Such loyalties are hard to find.

Our pets are entrusted to our care
Another way God's love is shared.

DEATH OF A PET

If you have ever lost a pet you loved
And then secretly questioned God above
You can truly understand the deep hurt and stress
When unconditional love they cannot express
Don't say tis only an animal to calm me down
Each holds a special spot and they are not around
Requiring so little, yet holding the key to our heart
Overjoyed with their eyes of love from the start
No more are the happy greetings each day
Only the empty loneliness that won't go away
A time to love and then comes goodbye
Just as humans, pets live and then they die
In the future across the bridge to rainbow land
We will reunite and the meeting will be grand
Just to hold, stroke and touch them once more
Will be an awesome occasion for sure!

MEMORIALS

One year has come and gone
Some days seem so very long
God knew there was no earthly cure
It broke our hearts, that's for sure.
We miss your happy, smiling face
Your memories we will never erase.
Someday God will call us to Heaven's shore
And we will be together forevermore!

10-4-24
8-20-05

Life was enjoyable to have you around
Whether mowing the lawn or tilling the ground
You gave us words of encouragement
And helping hands for accomplishments
Your happy smiles gave us hope
During life's trials to cope
All of these dear precious memories
Will sustain us through the years
We won't be early, we won't be late
Till we meet again at Heaven's Gate!

JUDY L CREEL

A heart of love stopped beating
Three years ago today
When God in His loving mercy
Called you away
They say time will heal all our sorrows
But we miss you more with each tomorrow
Life offers moments we would like to share
But with Heaven's grandeur, none would compare.

Life goes on, come whatever may
We miss you each and every day
Things are different without your life to share
You were someone who truly cared
Never too busy to lend a hand
And always there to understand
Your family was important to you
And you never wanted us to be blue
Someday in Heaven we'll meet again
We'll treasure your memories until then!

Another year has dawned
Five years have come and gone

It is not for us to reason why
We live and then of course we die

God is the giver of life and all
We are in his hands whate'er befall

We miss you, Dad, and feel so alone
One appointed day God will call us home

Forever, together we will be
Throughout all eternity

We will cherish your memories until then
Until we finally meet again

Today's your earthly birthday
We know you are better in every way
Heaven is now your eternal home
We will do our best to go on alone.
Broken is our family chain
One by one we will reunite again
God, please let him know we care
There is so much we'd like to share.
Our loved one is not forgotten—
Nor will he ever be
God will call us one by one to cross the sea
Then our family will be home eternally!

In my lifetime, I had a natural dad who loved me dearly.
When I married, I acquired a father-in-law who accepted
me sincerely.

Whenever and however either could assist me with a feat,
Both dads came to my aid in a heartbeat.

Neither could change the course of fate.
Time passed and now both have entered heaven's gate.

While on earth Bud worked hard and helped anyone in
need. Never looking for anything in return, he was a
friend indeed.

Church and family were both important to him.
We were so blessed to share in his wisdom.

Good memories will remain as husband, dad, grandpa,
and friend—till one by one, each of our lives will end.

Now Bud's enjoying the Heavenly Father's reign.
All because Jesus died and rose again.

On the Cross, Jesus paid our penalty for sin.
When our work on earth is done—we too can enter in.

JUDY L CREEL

No more noise on the top
of that old hill
Your tools no longer used,
just lay still.
Your big machines
no longer smoke and roar
The jumper cables
are strung no more.
A year has passed since your
family saw God call your name
At that second your body was healed,
your mind in the right frame.
Someday one by one your
family will cross that sea
We will join again in
Heaven and forever be.
All sickness and cares will
be a part of our past
We will enjoy Heaven's blessings
that will always last.

Again it's winter and the cold wind is blowing
Two years have passed since your home going

We miss you and so much we'd like to share
It's lonely without your presence and care

Trials and health problems are part of your past
Because Heaven offers perfect peace at last!

Your smiles we can no longer see
For you reside in eternity
Your wisdom and help so willing to share
Will never be forgotten by those who care
Problems and health issues all part of your past
We all await the day we will see you at last
Till then we will remember your love
Until we meet again in Heaven above

Four years have just elapsed
Day by day the time has passed
Losing a loved one is a hard transition
Not sure the task will ever come to fruition
We know you are enjoying Heaven's domain
But without you, our life is not the same!

God took you to Heaven five years ago
His physical healing for you to show
On earth you suffered pain and memory loss
Healing was not available at any cost
We are thankful you are in Heaven above
Enjoying all the benefits of God's Love
We certainly all miss you still
But are learning to accept God's will.

Mothers clean, cook, and do laundry
They are always caring for their family

Many moms are outgoing and a daily riot
But some like my mom were shy and quiet

When Dad got sick and passed away
Mom felt her life also ended that day

She never drove a car or worked outside the home
Belonged to any club and never lived alone

Long, endless hours encompassed her days
But she was faithful to read her Bible and pray

Then as her hearing and sight began to decrease
Any happiness and contentment began to cease

Immobility set in and caused her body much pain
Thus making her physical life difficult to maintain

Those of the family close by her side
Encouraged her to keep up her stride

Now her Savior has called her home
And Dad and Mom will no longer be alone

With their Savior they will live fulfilled forever
Because eternity in Heaven means parting never!

JUDY L CREEL

	Birth	Death
	10-4-24	8-20-05
	1-16-25	8-21-13

Often it seems like forever
since God called you both home.
Being an only child leaves me
feeling very alone.
Living next door was precious
when your presence was near.
As a close family you left me
memories dear.
The love and concern of good
parents can never be measured.
Only left are past events and
occasions to be treasured.
I'm trusting in God's word that
you are in Heaven above.
Your ailments all gone and you're
sharing in God's eternal love!

Loneliness visits me each day since you're gone
Our lives were spent helping each other along
Sadness frequently knocks on my heart's door
Reminding me your presence is no more
Sincere prayers got us through hard times to bear
And God did give us much happiness to share
Parting with parents is a hard pill to take
God's call gave physical relief for their sake
We are happy that you both suffer no more
And have faith we'll see you again on Heaven's shore!

JUDY L CREEL

RETIREMENT

With much prayer and partly due to health reasons
Pastor and Evie have made a retirement decision.

His accomplishments have reached far and wide
With his faithful wife, Evie, by his side.

All of our lives have been touched in countless ways
By their faithful service throughout the days.

The involvements in weddings, funerals, graduations
Have been much more than just a paid vocation.

Endless meetings and leading the Golden Heirs
Schedules and appointments have resulted in gray hairs.

His way of life has been lived with profound dedication
From the beginning to the end of every situation.

Many of the flock have already gone to Heaven above
Because of his steady proclamation of God's love.

Whether you call him Dad, Grandpa, Pastor, or friend,
There is a closeness that will never end.

His love of God, family, and friends is evident in his devotion
Applying God's word as needed with heartfelt emotion.

Pastor,
> As you visit and minister to those in need
> God will continue to use you indeed!
> Thank you so much for sharing God's love
> Many rewards will await you above!

WHAT IS RETIREMENT?

*R*ejoicing in God's blessings
*E*njoying life to the fullest
*T*rusting in God's provisions
*I*nteresting hobbies
*R*emembering others in prayer
*E*nvisioning the best is yet to come
*M*eeting new people
*E*njoying family and friends
*N*o definite schedule
*T*elling others of God's love!

It's a retirement party, they say
So let's enjoy this festive day

How our paths have crossed only Heaven knows
But that's how the events of life come and go

It's been great to get to know you and Rose
As you've preached God's words to keep us on our toes

We pray for God's blessings where'er he leads
And are confident He'll meet your needs

Please accept this little gift from us to you
We truly appreciate all the things you do

We won't be the last nor were we the first
To put a little *cha-ching* in your purse

The money won't make you healthy, wealthy, or wise
The fact that we will miss you is no disguise

Best wishes, happiness, and healthy days
These are the parting partitions we pray!

At S&T Bank I will no longer stay
As of December 1, I'll be on my way

Over a year ago my position they did eliminate
But retirement for me was a hard decision to validate

Each of you were like family to me
And with you I sincerely liked to be

Thirty-three-plus years of my life
Sharing laughter and sometimes strife

It was my personal joy getting to know you all
If any of you need anything, please give me a call

My life has been enriched by everyone
Customers and coworkers have been fun

Thank you so much from my heart
As a new page in my life I start

Only God knows what our futures hold in store
I pray each of you will enjoy blessings galore!

JUDY L CREEL

SEASONS

Snowflakes, snowflakes falling all around
Yet not one alike can be found.

Each is unique by God's own plan
Just as you and I were created by his hand.

Outside it's cold and the wind is blowing
Inside it's comfy and the fire is glowing.

Dirty dishes in the sink have a story to tell
While many go hungry, we are eating very well.

Nestled together with a roof over our heads
When it's time to retire, we have a warm, cozy bed.

We are so fortunate with people to love and food to eat
We have clothes to keep us warm and shoes for our feet.

May we appreciate these gifts from God's hand
And the privilege to live on America's land!

Old, ugly pine trees once lined my neighbor's hillside
As I looked out my front window, I could have cried
These trees would have never won a landscaping show
How they even managed to stand, I'll never know
Skinny, straggly, and branches missing
Oh that they could be gone, I was a-wishing

Then one day as I gazed about the sight a-grumbling
A storm went through, and the trees went a-tumbling
A beautiful sight has emerged on that hill
Hidden treasures revealed by God's will
How thankful I am as each new day dawns
To observe the awesome landscape since the trees are gone

This serves as a reminder to me
And I pray the people around me can see
Behind those heartaches we bear
God has a beautiful vision to share
Events will work out according to the plan of the Father
No need for me to get upset, worried, or bothered
I'll leave the circumstances of life to His way
Then I can be sure everything will be okay!

JUDY L CREEL

THE BLOSSOM

No blossom of life unfurls exactly the same
Each petal is to unfold to beauty not shame

The blossom blooms in various colors, shapes, and sizes
As the petals emerge by their choice foolish or wise

The strength of the blossom is in the vine
Each petal connected survives just fine

As the blossom continues to form
The petals can add beauty each morn

This blossom has a perfect design
That the petals can ruin or align

Each blossom is assigned a season in time
God affords our petals a chance to shine

If our petals fail to produce beauty each day
The blossom will restore and throw damage away

Connected to the vine the petals will be so fine
And make future blossoms in His beauty divine

When the season of petals is past
The blossom will bloom in Heaven and last

THE FALL SEASON

Hot, humid weather is slowly winding down
Swimming, picnics, and summer games no more abound

Weeding and mowing grass is coming to an end
As we notice leaves turning orange, yellow, and red

Only God's paintbrush could produce such a feat
His beautiful canvas no person can repeat

The months of September, October, and November, known to
us as fall
Is by far the loveliest season of all

The days are warm, and the nights are cool
Homes are quiet as the children return to school

Homework and football take center stage
As the season is enjoyed by folks of any age

Surrounded by pumpkins, cornstalks, and mums
Vegetables, apples, peaches, and plums

God's provisions are evident in the harvest we see
Oh, to be more thankful—you and me!

Let us not take for granted the things so richly provided
The life that God's hand has so faithfully guided.

JUDY L CREEL

Veterans Day Poem

Ponder the messages left for America from veterans who are dead
Or think about the agony from wounded veterans in hospital beds
Those soldiers who deal each waking moment with aggravation
Many in wheelchairs as a means of their normal transportation
Families' lives are all too often altered or shattered
Loved ones throughout the battlefields are scattered
As we enjoy our freedom, parades and celebrate
Let us not for a minute the cost devaluate
Fly that flag proudly so we will demonstrate
Freedom is never free by anyone's estimate
America is still the greatest and best country on earth
There is never a way under the sun to measure her worth!

Happy New Year

We know time stands still for no one
The old year's gone and New Year's come

All of our past is but a memory
Only God our future can see

Someone new could be added to the family tree
Someone else could be subtracted like you or me

Remember to multiply the blessings
Then divide by the troubles

Net income will always be a plus
If our life to God's hand we entrust!

JUDY L CREEL

January brings in a new calendar year
This offers to some happiness and others fear
The old year, no more to live, is gone
God knows what we did right and also our wrongs
He understands the joys we got to share
And the heartaches we had to bear
God in His mercy has extended more time
In love, desiring no soul be left behind

Another year has come and gone
And for us another year has dawned
This future year holds a new measure
Places, events, and happenings to treasure
It may be a year of blessedness
Or one that puts us to the test
As we fulfill our designated roles
We must remember God is in control

JUDY L CREEL

Has the worldwide economy left you wearing a frown?
As the bad news is spread all around the town

Be it summer, winter, springtime, or fall
Our Heavenly Father has control of it all

Money investments are looking dark and bleak,
But God is able to provide our needs in a blink

As the economy continues to look dismal and gray
And it appears that life savings are falling away

There's everlasting hope in the Father above
As we trust in his unchanging love

No reason to face each day with dismay
Our God has promised strength for the day

Let's reevaluate where we store our treasures
Are they for our pleasure, or do they meet God's measure?

Someday these concerns of life will all pass away
As we enter Heaven's pearly gate one glorious day

Temporaries on earth should cause no need for despair
We will walk on golden streets through Eternity there

Jesus paid the huge price for our entrance to be free
Have you accepted this gift on bended knee?

The most important decision on earth doesn't cost you a dime
Ask Jesus into your heart while there is still time!

SYMPATHY

SYMPATHY

A few words to let you know we care
And with you, your sorrows share
Prayers are offered on your behalf
For guidance down your path
God will somehow mend your broken heart
And only He can perform that part
If we can help you along the way
Remember, we are just a phone call away!

We want you to know that we do truly feel your pain
Life after losing a loved one is never the same

No one can erase the good memories you hold in your heart
As down this new way of life you are required to start

Somehow God enables us to continue down our path
And occasionally to muster a smile or a laugh

Please accept help from others each day
And we too are just a phone call away!

God's ways are not our ways
That's what the Bible says.
We know God never makes a mistake
But the tough trials are hard to take.
Praying He'll impart His guidance
For every future circumstance.
Your sorrow we share in our hearts
And our love we want to impart.
If we can help you in any way
Remember, we're just a phone call away!

Searching for special words to say
To help ease your heartache today

Death of our loved ones cause us loss and pain
But we will see them one day in Heaven's domain

Yet a little while, so hold tight, my friend
And it will be our turn to take that bend

We will be ushered into Heaven above
And once more see the ones we love

This blessed reunion will have no end
All because Jesus died and rose again

JUDY L CREEL

Oh how sad your heart is today
May it help in some small way

To know others share in your grief
For a life on earth that was so brief

Hold on to those memories so dear
It is all right to shed those tears

Remember we are always here for you
And offer help for anything we can do

It is so hard when sadness knocks on our door
We have all experienced heartaches for sure

This helps us to understand the pain you feel
The sympathy we extend is certainly real

We pray God will fill the void of death
And let you have some peaceful rest

Please know we do truly care
And our help we want to share

Let us know what we can do
To ease the pain and sorrow for you!

JUDY L CREEL

Humanly speaking, losing a loved one is hard to bear
Please know you are not alone as we and others care

We pray for sunshine in your life someday
As God lovingly rolls the dark clouds away

As your loved one has gone to Heaven above
Thus to be well and sharing in Eternal love

With the memories you are never alone
Guard them until your day to go home

It has been a long and hard road
As your family bore the load

God and your commitment held you all together
Thus, the sickness you were able to weather

Barb endured the pain and carried her cross
Now family and friends experience her loss

Her life was a wonderful testimony for all
Then God took away the hurt and gave the last call

Parents, George, Chris, Kelsey, and Josh
Only God can and will fill your deep loss

As family and friends say good-bye on this earth
Remember, Jesus paid full price for Heaven's worth

We will all see Barb someday in Heaven above
Via acceptance of God's precious gift of love!

JUDY L CREEL

THANK YOU

Thank You

I was introduced to you three years ago
Through an acquaintance we both know

It was in God's divine plan that our paths would one day meet
Getting to know you and share in your life has been a treat

God has blessed you with a caring heart
Which was evident from the very start

Your love for your family shines through
Despite the events that have been hard for you

Striving each week in the Awana class to do our best
Has had moments of challenge and put us to the test

As we endeavor to teach the Puggles about God's love
We realize we need the Heavenly help from above

Their attention span is short and energy level is full speed
I appreciated your help as we tried to plant the seed

Only God can make the seeds of his word grow in their hearts
Thanks again as we together faithfully did our part!

As sweet as the Puggles are in my heart
To manage all by myself, I'm not that smart

Planting the seed of God's word is an awesome task
Just trusting that some will grow in their hearts and last

Busy as our Puggles certainly can be
I needed your extra hand, you see

I appreciated you, my friend
Many thanks to you I extend!

WEDDING

A handsome groom and a beautiful bride
Today you repeat your vows side by side

You promise each other till death do you part
A lifelong commitment together you now start

This becomes the first day of the rest of your life
May God bless you with many years as husband and wife!

As you walk down the aisle and stand together at the altar
You are living the dream and think it is impossible to falter

The bride is wearing something new, something borrowed,
something blue
The groom is realizing after all this time his prayers have
come true

Today marks the day you promise to love, honor, and obey
Take to heart the words that seem so easy for you to say

May your wedding day be the start of something grand
As before family, friends, and God you stand

We pray all good times come your way
As you start to share your life today!

JUDY L CREEL

Protect your dreams for a lifetime and not just today
Do not let your hopes wither or vanish away

Keep the fire burning, and don't allow the flames to die
The grass being greener on the other side is a lie

Yes, you will definitely have good times and bad
Periods you are happy and days you are sad

As a couple always to each other hold tight
Be steadfast in your marriage and win the fight

Draw your strength and wisdom from the Lord above
And remember your precious feeling of love!

Mr. and Mrs. Jones are now a married pair
Partners in life with everything to share

Activities and events to enjoy together
With each other the storms of life to weather

Thank you for the invitation, we say
Congratulations on your wedding day!

JUDY L CREEL

Congratulations to the new husband and wife
Best of wishes as you begin your married life

It's wonderful to be part of your special event
Being so special to us, you know much love is sent!

Best wishes as you marry to the happy pair
It's a pleasure, your happiness to share

May the love you have for each other continue to grow
Building a lasting relationship, the world to show!

Happy first anniversary to Tirzah and Pete
One full year of married life complete

Looking back to the day you first met
You can be proud of your accomplishments

Stay close to each other and the Lord above
As you continue to enjoy His gift of love

Forget the problems and occasional tears
And pray God gives you many more years

Events for enjoyment and happenings to treasure
And hopefully blessings too numerous to measure

Happy Anniversary to the both of you
Congratulations as you celebrate year two
Life has a way of moving along so fast
A gift from God is our memories that last
As you review your two years of married life
Recall the happy times and forget any strife
Look forward as future years unfold
Anticipate the happiness that is yet untold!

JUDY L CREEL

MYSTERY
IN
MIRACLE TOWN

So often it seemed my dreams and aspirations would never become a reality. Now Look—The church is full of family and friends and the weather outside is sunny and a balmy 80 degrees. I am walking back down the aisle in a beautiful, cinderella wedding gown with the greatest man in the world holding my hand. From college friends to being introduced by Pastor Ron for the first time as "Mr & Mrs Joe Lawson". Yep—how cool is that?? After greeting each guest as they exited Christ Miracle Church, we are off to get our wedding pictures taken for a remembrance of this wonderful day. Our reception seemed to be enjoyed by all and the food was delicious. Now we are off to Disney World for a week long honeymoon!! Yahoo!

Living on cloud nine is great but as we move into our condo, reality sets in. Unpacking and much work is awaiting us. While I attempt to wade through the boxes, Joe goes off to his law office to do catch up. Life has a way of moving along and our first year anniversary appeared on the calendar. Wow—time does go quickly. Well, well—surprise and surprise==my not feeling so well was defined by the doctor as pregnant. We really had not planned on increasing our family so soon but we quickly learned this doesn't always need planning. This doctor of mine has a way of keeping the diagnosis going on and on. My next visit he informed us we were not just having one baby but two. Wow, what fun getting ready to welcome our babies. The nursery is ready and my baby bump is huge.

Joe and I are so proud of our healthy twin boys, Carter and Carson. We are now believers that good things do come in pairs. Such a wonderful experience watching our little boys grow and the joy and happiness they bring.

Nine years later we continue down our path as the Lawson Family, but time and events have changed our life forever.

It was a dreary, rainy evening as I exited the local grocery store. Not paying much attention to my surroundings, I quickly unloaded my grocery cart of the items into the back of my SUV. There was a nip in the air as the sun was beginning to set. As I am returning the shopping cart to the station, I notice a man out of the corner of my eye. He is a tall man in a black trench coat and seemed to be watching my every move. An eerie feeling caused me to walk a little faster back to my car. Once inside I took a deep breath and proceeded out of the lot and down the highway. The roads were wet and the lights of the oncoming cars are causing a glare. Who was that tall man in the black trench coat? Why did he make me feel so uncomfortable?? My uneasiness caused me a sleepless and restless night. I kept seeing him in my mind.

Morning finally comes and the normal rush begins in the Lawson home. Trying to get Carter and Carson out of bed and out the door to the school bus has always been a chore. I wave good bye to the boys who amazingly did catch their bus. Those boys, who are my reason for living, keep me so busy! Now I quickly run upstairs to finish getting ready for my job as a local news reporter. As a news reporter it's a new adventure everyday and I must admit I have an exciting career.

Since the boys dad was killed, I am so thankful for the income my job provides. This allows us to stay in our upscale condo and in the neighborhood we've grown to love. We share our lives with friends and families who live close by. No other place I'd rather live!

Actually in a few months the year anniversary of my one and only love and my children's Dad will roll around. As I recall the events, Joe was late coming home that evening. After further investigation, police found Joe in his law office. He was slumped over his desk with a single gun shot wound to his head. Unfortunately there were no witnesses and Joe's killer is still at large.

Who and why would someone want to kill Joe? He was a family man, loved his boys, and helped many people in his local law office. These thoughts flood my mind everyday.

It is getting late and I need to get to work. The week went quickly and as always the boys have Saturday morning basketball practice at the school gym and then plans with the neighborhood buddies. As for me, Patty, I get to clean and do laundry. Where in the world does all this dirty laundry come from?

Sunday has always been church attendance day and we have been long time active members of Christ Miracle Church down the street. The next church event is a big one.

Planning for the social at the church always requires much work from everyone. We look forward to collecting non-perishable food items and clothing for the needy every year. Also the carry in dinner for the members and workers is always a treat. Time has passed so quickly and this rather chilly morning makes the aromas of the food in the electric roasters and crockpots smell extra good. Also the array of baked goods available for purchase looks tempting. These people are such GOOD cooks!! The donations of clothing and food items are definitely larger than any year I can remember. It is wonderful to see the outpouring of love. OH NO—There is that man over at the entrance door to the fellowship hall. The tall man in the black trench coat. Pretty sure this is the same man I saw a few weeks ago in the grocery store parking lot. I froze as I watched him stack a box of canned goods on the donation table and then he quietly exited the building. Who is this man and why does he make me so uneasy? No one else, amid the flurry of activity, seemed to notice him or be bothered. Maybe I am just over sensitive but he gives me the jitters! Back to the task at hand. Such a busy day and a large supply of food and clothing has been collected for distribution to those in need. As clean up came to an end, we all left with thankful hearts. Carter and Carson were so tired but each expressed their satisfaction of the events as we drove home. Their Dad would have been so proud to see the hard work they so willingly offered to help others. Joe was so proud of his boys and displayed their pictures next to our wedding picture on his desk at the law office. He beamed when people commented that they looked like Daddy.

Sometimes life doesn't seem fair. Joe is not here to enjoy life but his killer is free! It is still so hard to accept and I definitely don't understand!

Waking up after a good night sleep is so refreshing Over breakfast the boys and I discussed the upcoming Christmas season. Of course there would be cookies to bake, gift shopping and tree trimming. My plans to make Christmas enjoyable for Carter and Carson were of utmost importance. Joe prided himself in choosing the perfect gifts for his boys. How will I ever fill his shoes?

The weekend again, and the boys are so excited as they have prepared for this seasons basketball tournament. No problem getting out of bed early this Saturday as they have hopes of becoming the champions for Miracle High. It has been a close game and everyone is on the edge of their seats as the final shot led Miracle High to the basketball championship and the victory for this season. Watching and cheering, my heart sank as I saw Carson fall to the floor after making the winning shot for his team. Amid the victory yells, screams and high fives Carson was assisted into the ambulance.

After Xrays were read and tense moments of waiting at the hospital, the doctor on duty reported "no broken bones just a bad sprain to the right ankle." The discharge nurse gave us a paper for pain medications and a list of necessary precautions. Now home for Carter and I to be nurse and care for the wounded.

JUDY L CREEL

What a weekend for the Lawson family!!
A new week and the boys are off to school with Carson on crutches.
They are still feeling pretty good about the championship title that is worth bragging about.

For me just another day in the life of a news reporter. We see the good and the bad. With the snow steadily falling the roads are becoming treacherous. Down the road I see two police cars with their lights flashing. As I approach the scene I can see a car down over the hillside at the entrance to the Miracle Mall. I pulled over into the parking lot just as I heard the siren of the ambulance arriving. It seemed impossible to get close enough for details. The paramedics were pulling a tall man out of the vehicle and putting him on a stretcher. From where I was standing-OH NO he is wearing a black trench coat. My mind is going crazy and I have an eerie feeling. Pretty sure this is the same man I saw at the grocery store parking lot and at the Church social. I really have the jitters now!! As the paramedics carried the body on the stretcher up the hillside, I can see they have already covered him with a sheet over his head. The coroner has arrived and will pronounce him dead at the scene. Who was this tall man with the black trench coat? Now I will never know!! I am leaving this spot to cover any other news worthy happenings I come upon. Fortunately the morning accident moved to the back of my mind as other events took center for news documentation.

After dinner, as was the Lawson family routine, the boys did their homework as I cleared the table and we always discussed our day. Just before retiring I picked up the local newspaper and the one obituary caught my eye. It was for a Paul Duitt who died as a result of a car accident by the Miracle Mall entrance. Wait a minute—that tall man in the black trench coat was Paul Duitt? Interesting—but I never heard that name before?? Why did I always respond with an eerie feeling? Who really was that tall man in the black trench coat?? Little was said in this obituary. Services were to be private, no close survivors only a niece and nephew and he was born in Wexton, Michigan. I never heard of that town! Everything had to be a crazy co=incidence—that's it—a crazy co-incidence!!

Hard to believe the Christmas season is past, boys back in school, and exactly one month till year anniversary of Joe's tragic death. Still no leads, no motives and police have reached a dead end. I am getting ready to go back to the news office after my two week vacation. I just met the new girl they hired to help in the news room. She seems very nice, but is quiet and stays in her cubicle most of the time. The office staff call her Joan. So Joan it is when I pass her cubicle at work. This evening the boys mentioned they hired a new janitor named Dan at school. Time passed and more information revealed that Joan and Dan were actually a married couple who moved to the area from Michigan.

Wanting to be hospitable as winter gave way to the spring season, I invited Joan & Dan for dinner. It was a nice evening and they seemed to enjoy the roast beef dinner. Conversation was light as we shared only a little about Joe's death and they shared a little about the sad story of the loss of their only son to a drug addiction. We learned there last name was Gola and they moved here to take care of an uncle.

Our friendship continued to grow not only at work, but Carter and Carson found a new role model in Dan. Dan welcomed the time he and the boys were playing basketball, riding ATV's, bowling, etc. Work kept Joan and I busy, but once in a while we treated ourselves to a shopping trip and dinner out. The Gola's joined the Christ Miracle Church and sat with us every Sunday. Summer found us swimming at the local pool every chance we got. That's where a mysterious comment was made that left me stunned. Joan said she and Dan were going back to Wexton for the weekend to take care of legal business. Wexton? Where did I come across that name? I grew weak as in my mind, I realized they were from the same town—But his name was Duitt—The tall man in the black trench coat???? Joan asked if I was all right and said "you look like you saw a ghost"!

JUDY L CREEL

I tried to make her believe I was fine, wished her a safe trip and quickly left the pool. My mind was in a spin—the obituary said Paul Duitt was from Wexton, Michigan—Dan & Jane Gola from Wexton??? Moved here to take care of an uncle—but he passed away? Could the uncle be Paul Duitt—the tall man in the black trench coat? Only survived by a niece & nephew—was he the man who died on the snowy road? I am so confused??? Why do I have the jitters? I need someone to explain this web in my mind! Why did Paul Duitt move to Miracle Town? I know I will need extra courage to ask Dan & Joan these questions "IF" they ever come back from Wexton again.

Not wanting to upset Carter and Carson I have purposely not mentioned the tall man in the black trench coat to them. I just kept going over and over the strange happenings and can not make any sense or connections. It is driving me crazy. Why do I feel so certain Dan & Joan are the missing link??

I was actually shocked that Joan came back from her weekend trip to Wexton and was in her cubicle on Monday at the News Room. I sent a text to the boys and they confirmed Dan the janitor was at the school, also. How will I ever approach these friends who came into our lives.

Weeks passed and I avoided the Golas. Carter and Carson started asking questions about the whereabouts of Dan & Joan. I answered with phoney excuses. I could not bring myself to ask Dan and Joan about this web in my mind. It had something to do with the tall man in the black trench coat. But what? How did this all fit together? It makes me so jittery inside, but I keep going over it in my mind—tall man-black trench coat?

One evening as I was sitting on my deck admiring the fall leaves that were turning yellow, red & orange, I heard someone walking up the yard. Deep in thought I was startled at the sight of Dan & Joan standing in front of my deck. They were forthright and ask "What happened to our friendship— why have you been ignoring us"? I could not hold in my tears any longer. Between sobs, I inquired if the uncle they spoke of was Paul Duitt. With a puzzled look they readily said "yes". They became so excited and asked how I met him. I tried to explain I never really met him but that confused them even more. Carter and Carson had joined us on the deck and wondered why I was crying along with being glad to see Dan & Joan. I guess it was time to let everyone know about the tall man in the black trench coat. I had their full attention as I shared the grocery store parking lot occasion, the church social when the tall man in the black trench coat donated the box of can goods and the fateful day he lost his life on the snowy road. I also shared I did not know him but I got an eerie feeling when I saw him. He gave me the jitters! But honest I never knew him. I continued to explain that reading his obituary helped me to realize he was the tall man in the black coat with only a niece and nephew as survivors. Dan & Joan confirmed this man was the uncle they moved to Miracle Town to help, but unfortunately he died in that car accident.

I had to know one more answer and I blurted out—What brought your uncle to Miracle Town"

They explained that their boy, Danny, was everything to Uncle Paul. Uncle Paul paid for Danny to go to rehab, bought him a car as a reward, thinking Danny was clean and free of drugs. Uncle Paul realized he was wrong the fateful night he got the terrible phone call from Danny informing his Uncle Paul he shot an attorney in Miracle Town. At that point they stopped talking and shock came over all of us. We realized that was Joe's killer. Everyone was crying—how could our friend's son be the killer of Joe and why? Dan explained that Uncle Paul said the attorney was to prosecute a drug dealer the next day according to Danny. Apparently this particular drug dealer was Danny's open line to his drug addiction. When the attorney refused to give him information needed to obtain more drugs, Danny shot him. Danny ended the phone call by telling Uncle Paul it was all over! Uncle Paul, as far as we know, nor us his parents have not seen Danny since that day.

JUDY L CREEL

To answer your question about our Uncle moving to Miracle Town, he had a mission. He wanted to find Danny or his body and also locate the attorney's family. His dream was to find closure of Danny and offer answers when he located the attorney's family. Unfortunately, our Uncle died with a broken heart that snowy morning!

After we digested some of this information, we realized we did receive closure and were able to thank God that our paths connected through His mysterious ways. Carter, Carson & I got answers to many unanswered questions, but what about Danny or his body?

I knew I had a new goal to solve the missing Danny dilema. Notifying the police of Joe's killer, we informed them of this missing killer. The authorities assured us they would continue the investigation.

The boys, Dan, Joan and I resumed spending time together and went to see the Christmas Play in a nearby town. On the way we enjoyed looking at the Christmas lights that seemed to shine brighter this year. Snowflakes were falling and softly coating the landscapes as we stopped at a classy dining spot and on to enjoy the Christmas Play. The story of baby Jesus always gives us hope and wonderment. Once again the Christmas Holidays were over and back to work and a New Year. Hard to believe the boys would be graduating this year from High School and then on to college! These are events Joe will never get to experience.

A few weeks later in the newspaper there was a local police release about body remains being located 50 miles north of Miracle Town in an abandoned mine. It was in a remote area far from the beaten path and at first thought to be animal remains by some local hunters. The body was badly decomposed so they were awaiting toxicology reports for possible identification. Time seems to stand still when you so despertly want answers. My heart ached for Dan & Joan as the days rolled into weeks. One night in the middle of summer, while we were all having dinner, a knock came to the front door. The police officer who was assigned the missing identity case of Danny was staring me straight in the eyes. He asked to talk to the Gola's. He informed them the remains found in the abandoned mine were those of their son, Danny Gola!

What a mixture and flood of emotions came forth from Dan & Joan, the boys and myself. All the past questions seemed to have answers or did they?

The Why questions remained—Why did these events have to happen? Why did this happen to our family? Why did they happen to Dan & Joan? These are questions left unanswered as we close this chapter of our lives. Truly the answered questions bonded people who were once strangers in a positive way.

Six years later life has once again altered our lives:

The day is perfect for graduation. Dan, Joan and I are enjoying a sunny 80 degree day as we witness a big event. Carter and Carson have fulfilled the qualifications to be certified, board approved, lawyers. Joe would have been so proud of the boys who have followed his footsteps. If only Danny could have taken a different path was in the back of all of our minds.

As for me, I am still working as a news reporter and residing in Miracle Town in the condo that has been home for twenty plus years!

JUDY L CREEL

SUMMARY

The author Judy's heart is touched by the love God shows in everyday life. Whatever the events in life, we never walk alone. We all need to be reminded—the number of years on earth is a short stay compared to eternity!

Judy resides in Kittanning, Pennsylvania, with her husband, Gary, dog, and two cats. A daughter, a son, and his wife complete the family. As a retired bank manager, she finds writing poetry a relaxing pastime. Her desire is that others will be blessed by reading these poems from her heart.